UNDERSTANDING ARTIFICIAL INTELLIGENCE CLASS V

DR DHEERAJ MEHROTRA

Contents

Preface

Dear Young Learners,

Welcome to the fascinating world of Artificial Intelligence (AI)! This book is designed especially for you, our curious Class V students, to help you understand what AI is and how it touches our lives magically daily. Have you ever wondered how your favourite voice assistant answers your questions or how your tablet shows you cartoons you might like? That's all because of AI! Through this book, we'll take you on an exciting journey to discover the amazing things AI can do and how it helps make our lives easier, smarter, and more fun.

In this book, you will Meet AI and learn how it thinks and works. Explore real-life examples of AI, like robots, innovative toys, and apps. Enjoy fun activities and colourful illustrations that make learning about AI simple and exciting. Learning about AI will spark your imagination and inspire you to think creatively about the future. So, let's dive into this wonderful world of Artificial Intelligence and have fun learning together. Happy Learning!

Author

CHAPTER I

Understanding Artificial Intelligence

Artificial Intelligence, or AI, is a technology that allows machines and computers to think, learn, and solve problems like humans. It's like giving a computer a brain!

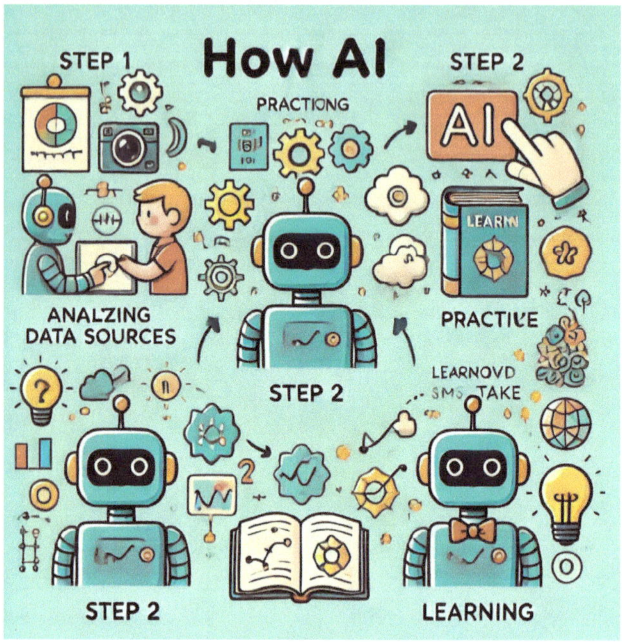

Artificial Intelligence, or AI, is a fascinating technology that empowers machines and computers to think, learn, and solve problems like humans.

How does AI work?

AI learns in a way that mirrors human learning processes. Just as you acquire knowledge and skills in school through practice and experience, AI systems utilize data to improve their performance over time.

This learning can occur through various methods, including:

Supervised Learning: *In this approach, AI is trained on a labelled dataset, where the correct output is provided for each input. The system learns to make predictions based on this training data.*

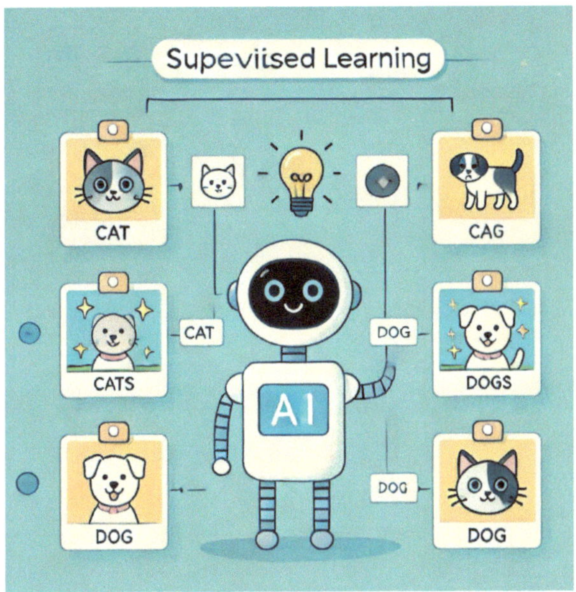

Unsupervised Learning: *AI is given data without explicit instructions on what to do with it. The system identifies patterns and structures within the data independently.*

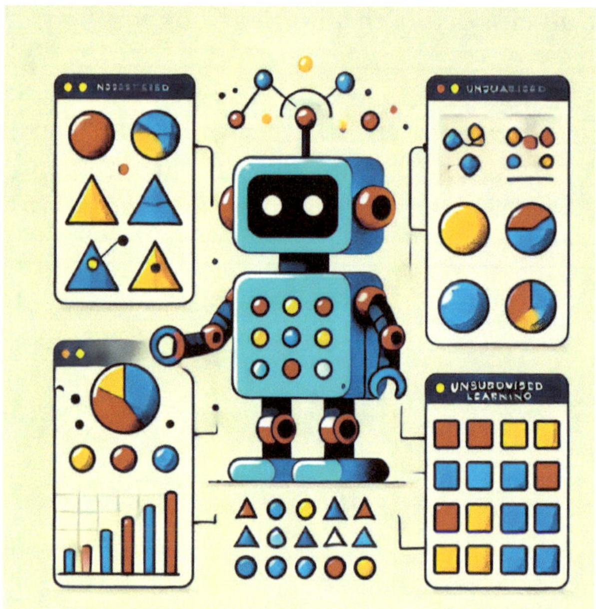

***Reinforcement Learning** involves training AI through trial and error. The system receives rewards or penalties based on its actions, allowing it to learn optimal behaviours over time.*

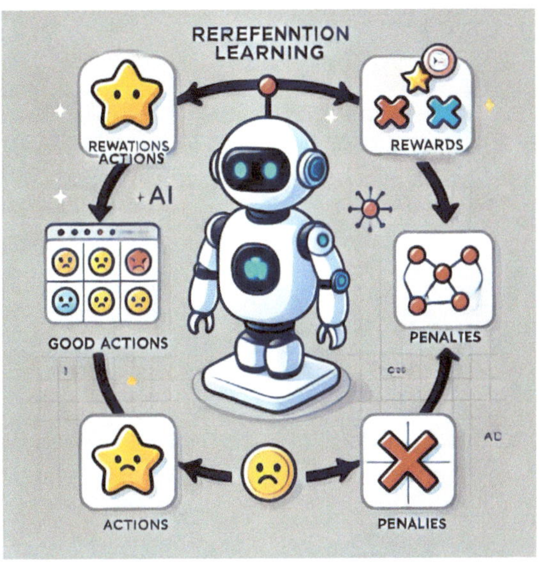

AI Learning:

Through these learning techniques, AI can adapt to new information, improve its decision-making capabilities, and perform tasks once thought exclusive to human intelligence.

AI is a powerful tool miming human cognitive functions, making it an integral part of modern technology. As we continue to explore its potential, we can expect even more innovative applications that will shape our future.

Example: Imagine teaching a robot to recognize animals. You show it pictures of cats and dogs. Over time, the robot learns to tell them apart by noticing differences, like pointy ears for cats and floppy ears for dogs.

The Future of AI

AI is constantly improving and can do amazing things. In the future, it might help build innovative, eco-friendly cities or discover new medicines.

Artificial Intelligence is an incredible technology that is changing the world. Understanding and using AI wisely can make our lives better and more exciting. Always remember to use AI responsibly and keep learning how it works—who knows, you might one day create the next significant AI invention!

• • •

Short Solved Questions

Question 1: What is Artificial Intelligence (AI)?

Answer: AI technology allows machines and computers to think, learn, and solve problems like humans.

Question 2: How does AI help in our daily lives?

Answer: AI helps play games, assists doctors, and even drives cars.

Question 3: How does AI learn?

Answer: AI learns by using data to improve its performance over time, similar to how humans learn through practice and experience.

Question 4: What is supervised learning in AI?

Answer: In supervised learning, AI is trained on a labelled dataset with the correct output for each input.

Question 5: What does unsupervised learning involve?

Answer: Unsupervised learning involves giving AI data without explicit instructions, allowing it to identify patterns and structures independently.

Question 6: What is reinforcement learning?

Answer: Reinforcement learning involves training AI through trial and error, using rewards or penalties to teach optimal behaviours.

Question 7: How does AI improve its decision-making capabilities?

Answer: AI adapts to new information and uses supervised, unsupervised, and reinforcement learning to improve decision-making.

Question 8: Can you give an example of AI learning?

Answer: A robot can learn to recognize animals by analyzing pictures of cats and dogs, noticing differences like pointy ears for cats and floppy ears for dogs.

Question 9: What is one potential future application of AI?

Answer: AI might help build smart and eco-friendly cities.

Question 10: How can AI impact medicine in the future?

Answer: AI could help discover new medicines and improve healthcare.

Question 11: Why is it essential to understand AI?

Answer: Understanding AI helps us use it wisely to improve our lives and explore its innovative applications.

Question 12: How does AI mimic human intelligence?

Answer: AI mimics human cognitive functions like learning, problem-solving, and decision-making.

Question 13: What is an example of reinforcement learning?

Answer: Training a robot to complete a task by rewarding good actions and penalizing mistakes is an example of reinforcement learning.

Question 14: What makes AI a powerful tool?

Answer: AI's ability to adapt, learn, and perform tasks once exclusive to human intelligence makes it a powerful tool.

Question 15: What should we remember when using AI?

Answer: We should use AI responsibly and keep learning how it works to use its potential best.

CHAPTER II

AI in Our Daily Lives

AI in Our Daily Lives: AI is all around us, helping in many ways. Here are some examples:

Voice Assistants: Tools like Siri and Alexa can answer questions, play music, or tell jokes.

Smartphones: AI helps make your photos look better and guesses what you want to type.

Games: AI acts like a brilliant opponent in video games, making them more exciting.

Shopping Apps: AI suggests items you might like based on your previous purchase.

Maps: AI shows the best routes to avoid traffic and reach your destination faster.

Smart Home Devices: One of the most visible applications of AI in daily life is through smart home devices. Products like smart speakers, thermostats, and security systems utilize AI to learn user preferences and automate tasks. For instance, smart thermostats can adjust the temperature based on your habits, while smart speakers can play music, set reminders, or control other smart devices through voice commands.

Personal Assistants: AI-powered personal assistants, such as Siri, Google Assistant, and Alexa, have revolutionized how we interact with technology. These assistants can answer questions, manage schedules, and even control smart home devices, making our lives more convenient. Their understanding of natural language and context allows for a more intuitive user experience.

Health and Fitness: AI applications are becoming increasingly prevalent in health and fitness. Wearable devices like fitness trackers and smartwatches use AI algorithms to monitor physical activity, heart rate, and sleep patterns. This data can help users make informed decisions about their health and wellness, providing personalized recommendations for exercise and nutrition.

Transportation: AI is also transforming the transportation sector. Ride-sharing apps like Uber and Lyft utilize AI to optimize routes and efficiently match passengers with drivers. Additionally, advancements in autonomous vehicles are paving the way for a future where self-driving cars could become a standard mode of transportation, potentially reducing traffic accidents and improving mobility.

Entertainment: AI plays a significant role in content recommendation systems in the entertainment industry. Streaming services like Netflix and Spotify use AI algorithms to analyze user preferences and viewing habits, suggesting movies, shows, and music tailored to individual tastes. This personalization enhances user engagement and satisfaction.

Challenges and Considerations: While AI offers numerous benefits, it also presents challenges that must be addressed. Privacy concerns arise as AI systems collect and analyze vast amounts of personal data. Additionally, there are ethical considerations regarding job displacement and the need for transparency in AI decision-making processes.

Why is AI Important? AI makes our lives easier, faster, and more fun! It helps solve problems, saves time, and improves health care and education. However, we must also use AI responsibly to ensure it is helpful and safe for everyone.

• • •

Solved Short Questions

Question 1: How does AI help with voice assistants?

Answer: AI enables tools like Siri and Alexa to answer questions, play music, or tell jokes.

Question 2: What does AI do in smartphones?

Answer: AI helps make photos look better and guesses what you want to type.

Question 3: How does AI make video games more exciting?

Answer: AI is an intelligent opponent, making games challenging and fun.

Question 4: What does AI do in shopping apps?

Answer: AI suggests items you might like based on what you've bought before.

Question 5: How does AI help with maps?

Answer: AI shows the best routes to avoid traffic and reach your destination faster.

Question 6: Give an example of AI in everyday life.

Answer: AI in voice assistants like Siri or Alexa helps answer questions and play music.

Question 7: Why is AI important for solving problems?

Answer: AI helps solve problems quickly and efficiently, making life easier.

Question 8: How does AI save time?

Answer: AI completes tasks faster, such as showing the quickest route on a map.

Question 9: How does AI improve health care?

Answer: AI helps doctors diagnose diseases and suggest treatments more accurately.

Question 10: What is one way AI improves education?

Answer: AI makes learning fun by providing personalized tools and activities.

Question 11: Why should we use AI responsibly?

Answer: Using AI responsibly ensures it is helpful, safe, and fair for everyone.

Question 12: How does AI guess what you want to type on your smartphone?

Answer: AI learns from your typing habits and predicts your next word.

Question 13: What makes AI-powered games more fun?

Answer: AI opponents make the game challenging by acting like real players.

Question 14: How does AI in shopping apps help you?

Answer: AI suggests items you might like, making shopping easier and more personalized.

Question 15: What is the overall benefit of AI in our daily lives?

Answer: AI makes life easier, faster, and more fun by solving problems and saving time.

CHAPTER III

How AI Helps the World

How AI Helps the World?

In Hospitals

AI is revolutionizing healthcare by assisting doctors in diagnosing diseases more quickly and accurately. With advanced algorithms and machine learning, AI can analyze medical images, patient data, and historical records to identify patterns that may indicate health issues. This speeds up the diagnostic process and suggests personalized treatment plans, ultimately leading to better patient outcomes.

In Schools

In the educational sector, AI is making learning more engaging and interactive. Various applications and tools powered by AI adapt to individual learning styles, providing personalized experiences for students. From intelligent tutoring systems to gamified learning platforms, AI fosters a fun and effective learning environment, helping students quickly grasp complex concepts.

In Nature

AI plays a crucial role in environmental conservation by tracking wildlife and monitoring ecosystems. Using drones and sensors, AI can gather data on animal populations and their habitats, enabling conservationists to make informed decisions. Additionally, AI helps protect forests by detecting illegal logging activities and predicting potential threats to biodiversity.

In Space

AI technologies have greatly enhanced the exploration of outer space. Scientists utilize AI to analyze vast amounts of data collected from telescopes and space missions, helping them to discover new planets and stars. AI algorithms assist in navigating spacecraft, optimizing routes, and even predicting cosmic events, making space exploration more efficient and insightful.

Economic Growth

Integrating AI into various industries drives economic growth by increasing productivity and creating new job opportunities. Automating repetitive tasks allows human workers to focus on more strategic and creative endeavours. Moreover, AI fosters innovation by enabling businesses to analyze market trends and consumer behaviour, leading to the development of new products and services that meet evolving demands.

Education Enhancement

AI is transforming education by providing personalized learning experiences. Intelligent tutoring systems adapt to individual student needs, offering tailored resources and feedback. AI also streamlines administrative tasks for educators, allowing them to dedicate more time to teaching and mentoring. Furthermore, AI-powered platforms facilitate access to quality education in remote areas, bridging the gap for underserved populations.

Safety and Security

AI enhances safety and security across various domains. In cybersecurity, AI algorithms detect and respond to threats in real time, protecting sensitive data from breaches.

• • •

Solved Short Questions

Question 1: How does AI assist doctors in healthcare?

Answer: AI helps doctors diagnose diseases quickly and accurately by analyzing medical images, patient data, and historical records.

Question 2: What is one benefit of AI in hospitals?

Answer: AI speeds up the diagnostic process and suggests personalized treatment plans, improving patient outcomes.

Question 3: How does AI make learning fun for students?

Answer: AI provides personalized learning experiences and uses intelligent tutoring systems and gamified platforms to make learning engaging.

Question 4: What role does AI play in environmental conservation?

Answer: AI tracks wildlife, monitors ecosystems, and detects illegal logging to help protect biodiversity and forests.

Question 5: How is AI used in space exploration?

Answer: AI analyzes telescope data, helps discover new planets, navigates spacecraft, and predicts cosmic events.

Question 6: How does AI contribute to economic growth?

Answer: AI increases productivity, automates repetitive tasks, and fosters innovation by analyzing market trends and consumer behaviour.

Question 7: What is one way AI enhances education?

Answer: AI provides personalized tutoring systems that adapt to individual student needs, making learning more effective.

Question 8: How does AI help educators in schools?

Answer: AI streamlines administrative tasks, allowing educators to focus more on teaching and mentoring students.

Question 9: How does AI facilitate education in remote areas?

Answer: AI-powered platforms provide access to quality education, bridging the gap for underserved populations.

Question 10: How does AI improve safety in cybersecurity?

Answer: AI detects and responds to threats in real time, protecting sensitive data from breaches.

Question 11: What is the role of AI in public safety?

Answer: AI helps law enforcement agencies predict and prevent crime, improving community safety.

Question 12: How does AI improve transportation safety?

Answer: AI in autonomous vehicles reduces accidents and enhances traffic management.

Question 13: What tools does AI use to monitor ecosystems?

Answer: AI uses drones and sensors to gather animal population and habitat data.

Question 14: How does AI optimize routes in space exploration?

Answer: AI assists in navigating spacecraft and optimizing routes for efficiency and accuracy.

Question 15: How does AI support businesses in innovation?

Answer: AI enables businesses to analyze market trends and consumer behaviour, which can lead to developing new products and services.

CHAPTER IV

Using AI Responsibly

AI is a fantastic tool that can help us in many ways, but we must use it responsibly to stay safe.

Here are some simple tips for using AI safely, explained with examples:

1. Be Smart Online: Never share your details with apps or websites, like your name, address, or phone number.

Example: If a chatbot asks, "What's your address?" you should reply, "I can't share that information!" Instead, you can enjoy chatting with the AI without giving it personal details.

Why It's Important: Sharing private information can be risky. By being cautious, you stay safe while using AI tools.

2. Ask an Adult

If unsure about an AI tool, ask a parent, teacher, or other trusted adult for help.

Example: You find a new drawing app and want to use it. Before downloading, ask your parents, "Is this app safe to use?" Your teacher can guide you in using AI tools safely for learning and schoolwork.

Why It's Important: Adults can help you choose safe and age-appropriate tools, ensuring you have a positive experience with AI.

3. Use it for Good

AI should be used to learn, play, and help others. Please don't use it to cheat, hurt feelings, or do anything harmful.

Example: Suitable Use: Use AI to solve a math problem by asking, "What is 12 divided by 4?" Copying answers from AI for homework without trying to learn yourself.

• • •

Solved Short Assignments

Question 1: What should you never share with apps or websites?
Answer: You should never share personal details like your name, address, or phone number.

Question 2: What should you reply if a chatbot asks for your address?
Answer: You should reply, "I can't share that information!"

Question 3: Why is it important not to share private information online?
Answer: Sharing private information can be risky and lead to unsafe situations.

Question 4: What should you do if you find a new AI tool and are unsure about it?
Answer: You should ask a parent, teacher, or trusted adult if the tool is safe.

Question 5: How can your teacher help you with AI tools?
Answer: Teachers can guide you in using AI tools safely for learning and schoolwork.

Question 6: What is an example of using AI for good?

Answer: Using AI to solve a math problem, like asking, "What is 12 divided by 4?"

Question 7: What is an example of misusing AI?

Answer: Copying answers from AI for homework without trying to learn yourself.

Question 8: Why is it important to use AI for good?

Answer: Using AI for good makes learning fun and ensures everyone benefits.

Question 9: What are three things you can use AI for good?

Answer: Solving math problems, learning a new fact, and creating art.

Question 10: Why is asking an adult about an AI tool helpful?

Answer: Adults can help you choose safe and age-appropriate tools, ensuring a positive experience.

Question 11: How can you practice staying safe with chatbots?

Answer: Pretend to chat with a chatbot and practice saying, "I can't share that" if it asks for personal information.

Question 12: What activity can you do to check the safety of an AI tool?

Answer: Find an AI tool online and discuss it with a parent or teacher before using it.

Question 13: What does it mean to "be smart online"?

Answer: It means not sharing personal details like your name or address with apps or websites.

Question 14: Why are these tips for using AI safely important?

Answer: They help protect your information, ensure the positive use of AI, and allow you to have fun safely.

Question 15: What can following these tips help you do?

Answer: It helps you enjoy AI safely, learn new things, and explore AI tools responsibly.

CHAPTER V

Fun with AI

Artificial Intelligence (AI) can make learning and playing super fun! Let's explore some exciting ways you can use AI daily.

Here are three fun activities you can try, with simple examples to help you understand them better.

1. Chat with AI

What to Do:
Use a chatbot to ask questions, tell stories, or even play text-based games.

Example: Ask an AI assistant like Alexa or Google Assistant questions like, "What's the capital of India?" or "Tell me a joke."

Use a chatbot app like ChatGPT to create a fun story together, such as about a superhero or an animal adventure.

Why It's Fun: AI chatbots are like talking to a smart friend who knows much about the world and can even make you laugh!

2. Play Games

What to Do: Play games where AI is your opponent. It can make the game exciting and challenging.

Example: Tic-Tac-Toe: Play against an AI and see if you can win.

Chess: Apps like Chess.com let you play against AI of different skill levels so you can improve your strategy.

Racing Games: AI drives the other cars, making the race thrilling.

Why It's Fun: AI opponents think differently every time, so the games stay exciting and unpredictable.

3. Try AI Drawing Apps

What to Do: Use AI-powered drawing tools to create amazing art or turn your rough sketches into polished pictures.

Example: AutoDraw: Draw a rough shape, and the AI will turn it into a neat picture, like a tree, house, or animal.

Colorfy: Use AI coloring apps to paint vibrant pictures.

DoodleMagic AI: Let the AI complete your doodles and turn them into creative designs.

Why It's Fun: AI drawing apps let you create art quickly and easily, even if you're not an expert artist!

Chat with AI: Open your voice assistant or download a chatbot app.

Play Games: Use game apps or visit websites like Chess.com or Quick, Draw! by Google.

AI Drawing Apps: Search for AutoDraw or other free drawing tools online.

Activity Challenge for You

Chat Challenge: Ask an AI assistant to tell you a story about a magical robot.

Game Challenge: Play Tic-Tac-Toe against AI and try to win three times in a row.

Drawing Challenge: Use AutoDraw to create a beautiful park scene with trees, birds, and swings.

Illustrations to Help You Visualize

A child talking to a smart speaker (Chat with AI).

A cheerful scene of kids playing a game with an AI opponent (Play Games).

• • •

Short Solved Questions

Question 1: Name one way you can use a chatbot for fun.

Answer: You can ask a chatbot like Alexa or Google Assistant to tell you a joke or answer questions like, "What's the capital of India?"

Question 2: What makes playing games with AI fun?

Answer: AI opponents think differently every time, so the games stay exciting and unpredictable.

Question 3: What can you do with an app like AutoDraw?

Answer: You can draw a rough shape, and the AI will transform it into a polished picture, such as a tree.

Question 4: What story could you ask an AI assistant to create?

Answer: You could ask it to create a story about a magical robot or a superhero adventure.

Question 5: What game can you play against AI to improve your strategy?

Answer: You can play chess against AI using apps like Chess.com.

Question 6: What is an idea for a picture you can create using AutoDraw?

Answer: You can create a park scene with trees, birds, and swings.

Question 7: Why are AI drawing apps helpful even if you're not an expert artist?

Answer: AI drawing apps let you create art quickly and easily by polishing your rough sketches.

Question 8: What type of AI-powered game lets you race against AI-controlled cars?

Answer: Racing games use AI to drive the other cars, making the race thrilling.

Question 9: Why is chatting with AI like talking to a smart friend?

Answer: AI chatbots know much about the world and can tell jokes, answer questions, and create stories.

Question 10: What is the first step to using AI drawing apps?

Answer: Find free online drawing tools like AutoDraw or Colorfy and start creating art.

Types of AI

Artificial Intelligence (AI) is like a super-smart helper that works differently. To simplify, let's look at the three main types of AI and how they are used. Think of them as levels of intelligence!

1. Narrow AI (Weak AI)

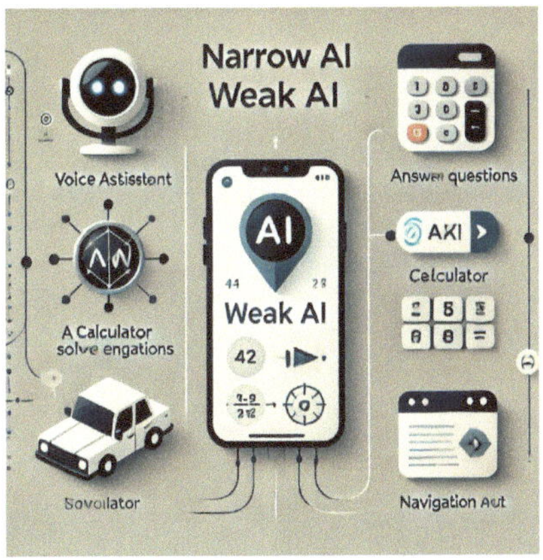

Narrow AI is smart at doing one specific thing well, but it can't do other tasks outside its area of expertise.

Examples: Siri or Alexa can answer your questions without cooking food or riding a bike. A calculator is great at solving math problems but doesn't know how to play games.

Why It's Useful: Narrow AI helps us with tasks like answering questions, recognizing faces, or showing the best route on a map.

2. General AI (Strong AI)

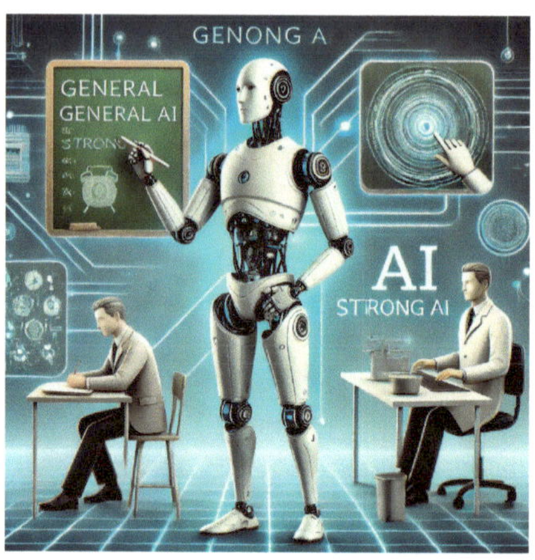

General AI is smarter than Narrow AI because it can do many things like a human. It can learn, solve problems, and make decisions independently.

Examples: Imagine a robot that can learn to play games, cook food, and help you with homework.

Why It's Special: General AI is still in development, but one day, it could perform many tasks like humans.

3. Super AI

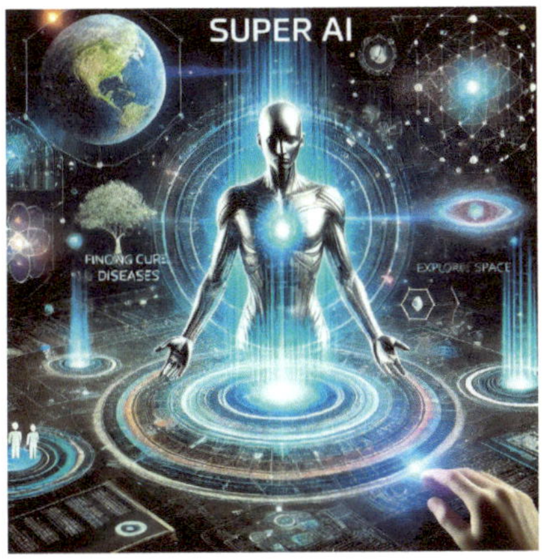

Super AI is the smartest of all. It can think, learn, and solve problems even better than humans!

Examples: A super AI robot might be able to find cures for diseases, explore distant planets, and build amazing things we haven't even imagined yet.

Why It's Fascinating: *Super AI doesn't exist yet, but scientists are working on making AI smarter every day.*

How Do These Types Work Together?

Currently, most of the AI we use is Narrow AI, such as the apps and tools we use daily. General AI and Super AI are ideas for the future, and they could make life even more exciting and manageable for everyone!

A Fun Way to Remember the Types

Narrow AI: Think of a pencil—it does one job well.

General AI: Like your teacher—it can do many tasks.

Super AI: Imagine a superhero who can do everything better than anyone else!

• • •

Short Answer Questions

Question 1: What is Narrow AI also called?

Answer: Narrow AI is also called Weak AI.

Question 2: What can Narrow AI do?

Answer: Narrow AI is very good at doing one specific task.

Question 3: Give an example of Narrow AI.

Answer: Siri or Alexa can answer questions but not cook food or ride a bike.

Question 4: Why is Narrow AI useful?

Answer: Narrow AI helps with tasks like answering questions, recognizing faces, or showing the best route on a map.

Question 5: What makes General AI different from Narrow AI?

Answer: General AI can do many tasks like humans, while Narrow AI specializes in one task.

Question 6: What is an example of General AI?

Answer: A robot that can play games, cook food, and help with homework is an example of General AI.

Question 7: Why is General AI unique?

Answer: General AI is still in development but could one day perform many tasks like humans.

Question 8: What is Super AI?

Answer: Super AI is the most intelligent type of AI. It can think, learn, and solve problems better than humans.

Question 9: Give an example of what Super AI could do.

Answer: Super AI might find cures for diseases, explore distant planets, and build amazing things.

Question 10: Does Super AI exist yet?

Answer: Super AI does not exist yet, but scientists are working on it.

Question 11: What type of AI do we mostly use today?

Answer: We mainly use Narrow AI today.

Question 12: How do Narrow AI, General AI, and Super AI differ in intelligence?

Answer: Narrow AI does one task well, General AI can do many tasks, and Super AI is more intelligent than humans.

Question 13: How can you remember Narrow AI?

Answer: Think of a pencil—it does one job well.

Question 14: How can you remember General AI?

Answer: Like your teacher—it can do many tasks.

Question 15: How can you remember Super AI?

Answer: Imagine a superhero who can do everything better than anyone else!

CHAPTER VII

Robots in Daily Life

Robots in Daily Life

Robots are amazing machines that can help us in many ways. With the help of Artificial Intelligence (AI), robots are becoming more innovative and more helpful in our daily lives. Let's see how robots with AI make our lives easier and more exciting!

1. Robots That Clean

Some robots, like robotic vacuum cleaners, use AI to clean floors without anyone helping them. They can move around furniture and even avoid falling down stairs.
Example: RoboVac is a robot that cleans your house while you play or do homework.

2. Robots in Restaurants

In some restaurants, robots deliver food to your table. AI helps them understand the restaurant's layout and find the correct table. Example: A robot waiter brings you your pizza with a smile!

3. Robots in Factories

AI-powered robots are used in factories to make cars, toys, and even computers. They can work quickly and precisely, helping create products faster. Example: An assembly line robot uses AI to assemble car parts.

4. Robots in Hospitals

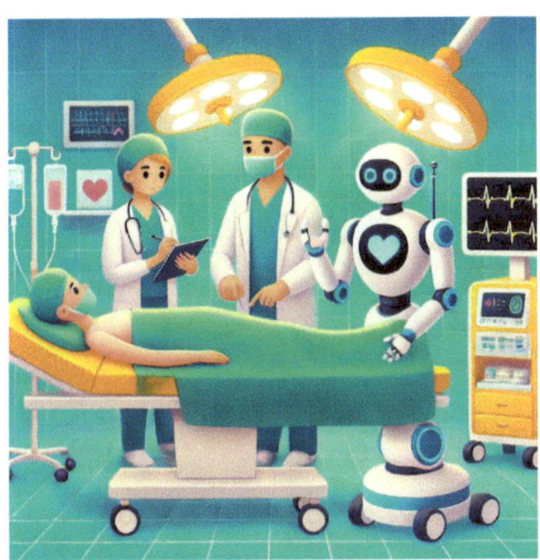

AI robots assist doctors by performing delicate surgeries or delivering medicines to patients. They are trained to work carefully and accurately. Example: A robot surgeon helps doctors during complex operations.

5. Robots for Fun

Some robots are made just for fun! AI-powered robots can play games, tell jokes, and even dance with you.
Example: A robot like Cozmo plays games and learns your favourite moves.

6. Robots That Help Nature

AI-powered robots can plant trees, remove plastic from oceans, and track endangered animals to keep them safe. Example: AI robots plant seeds in fields to help grow more crops.

•••

Solved Short Answer Questions

Question 1: What do robotic vacuum cleaners do?

Answer: Robotic vacuum cleaners use AI to clean floors, move around furniture, and avoid falling down stairs.

Question 2: Give an example of a robot that cleans.

Answer: RoboVac is a robot that cleans your house while you play or do homework.

Question 3: How do robots in restaurants help?

Answer: Restaurant robots deliver food to tables using AI to understand the layout and find the correct table.

Question 4: Give an example of a robot used in a restaurant.

Answer: A robot waiter delivers food, like pizza, with a smile.

Question 5: What tasks do robots in factories perform?

Answer: Factory robots make cars, toys, and computers by working quickly and precisely.

Question 6: How do assembly line robots use AI?

Answer: Assembly line robots use AI to assemble car parts efficiently.

Question 7: How do robots assist doctors in hospitals?

Answer: AI robots perform delicate surgeries and deliver medicines to patients.

Question 8: Give an example of a robot used in hospitals.

Answer: A robot surgeon helps doctors during complex operations.

Question 9: What are robots used for fun?

Answer: Fun robots play games, tell jokes, and even dance with you.

Question 10: Give an example of a fun robot.

Answer: A robot like Cozmo plays games and learns your favourite moves.

Question 11: How do AI robots help nature?

Answer: AI robots plant trees, remove plastic from oceans, and track endangered animals.

Question 12: What is an example of a robot helping nature?

Answer: AI robots plant seeds in fields to help grow more crops.

Question 13: What makes robots more intelligent and helpful daily?

Answer: Artificial Intelligence (AI) makes robots more innovative and functional.

Question 14: How do some robots respond like a real friend?

Answer: Some robots can recognize your voice and answer your questions.

Question 15: Why are robots in factories important?

Answer: Robots in factories help create products faster and with precision.

CHAPTER VIII

Applications of AI

Artificial Intelligence (AI) is like a super-smart helper that can make our lives easier, faster, and more fun!

Here are some of the key benefits of AI:

1. Saves Time

AI can do tasks quickly, helping us save time. Example: AI assistants like Siri or Alexa can instantly set reminders, find information, or play music.

2. Improves Healthcare

AI helps doctors find diseases early, suggest treatments, and even perform surgeries with precision. Example: AI analyzes X-rays to detect illnesses faster.

3. Makes Learning Fun

AI-powered apps and tools excite education by providing games, videos, and personalized learning experiences. Example: Apps like Duolingo help you learn new languages with fun activities.

4. Helps in Daily Life

AI is used in maps to find the fastest routes, smart cameras to take better photos, and shopping apps to suggest products. Example: Google Maps shows you the quickest way to a friend's house.

5. Creates Safer Environments

AI can predict weather disasters, monitor security cameras, and even assist in self-driving cars to avoid accidents. Example: AI alerts people about upcoming storms, helping them stay safe.

6. Solves Complex Problems

AI can handle significant challenges, like discovering new medicines or exploring space. Example: AI helps scientists analyze data to develop treatments for diseases.

7. Makes Games Exciting

AI is a competent opponent in video games, making them challenging and fun. Example: AI in racing games competes like a real player.

8. Protects Nature

AI helps track animals, protect forests, and reduce pollution. Example: AI-powered drones monitor wildlife to prevent poaching.

9. Boosts Creativity

AI helps create art, music, and even stories. It supports people in expressing their creativity. Example: Tools like AutoDraw turn simple sketches into beautiful designs.

10. Supports People with Disabilities

AI assists people with visual, hearing, or mobility challenges through tools like speech recognition or navigation aids. Example: AI-powered apps read out text for visually impaired users.

• • •

Solved Short Answer Questions

Question 1: How does AI save time?
Answer: AI can do tasks quickly, such as setting reminders, finding information, or playing music instantly.

Question 2: Give an example of how AI improves healthcare.
Answer: AI analyzes X-rays to detect illnesses faster and suggests treatments.

Question 3: How does AI make learning fun?
Answer: AI-powered apps provide games, videos, and personalized learning experiences.

Question 4: What is an example of an AI-powered learning app?
Answer: Apps like Duolingo help you learn new languages with fun activities.

Question 5: How does AI help in daily life?
Answer: AI finds the fastest routes on maps, improves photos with smart cameras, and suggests products in shopping apps.

Question 6: What is an example of AI helping in daily life?
Answer: Google Maps shows you the quickest way to a friend's house.

Question 7: How does AI create safer environments?
Answer: AI predicts weather disasters, monitors security cameras, and assists in self-driving cars to reduce accidents.

Question 8: Give an example of how AI keeps people safe.
Answer: AI alerts people about upcoming storms, helping them stay safe.

Question 9: What complex problems can AI solve?
Answer: AI helps discover new medicines and explore space.

Question 10: How does AI assist scientists?

Answer: AI analyzes data to develop treatments for diseases.

Question 11: How does AI make games more exciting?

Answer: AI is a competent opponent, making games challenging and fun.

Question 12: What is an example of AI in video games?

Answer: AI in racing games competes like a real player.

Question 13: How does AI protect nature?

Answer: AI tracks animals, protects forests, and reduces pollution.

Question 14: What is an example of AI helping the environment?

Answer: AI-powered drones monitor wildlife to prevent poaching.

Question 15: How does AI support people with disabilities?

Answer: AI provides tools like speech recognition and navigation aids, such as apps that read out text for visually impaired users.

CHAPTER IX

AI Ethics

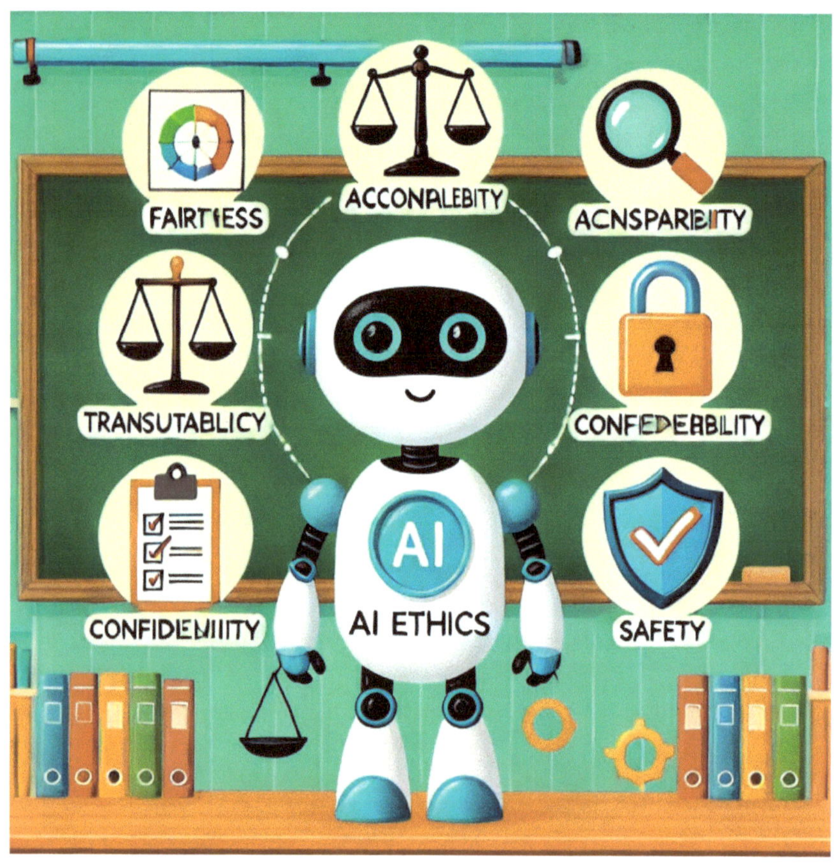

Ethics for Artificial Intelligence

What does AI Ethics suggest?

AI should treat everyone equally regardless of where they come from, their appearance, or how they talk.

Legal responsibility:

Those who are responsible for the creation and usage of artificial intelligence are the ones who must accept accountability for its actions. If artificial intelligence makes a mistake, they are required to correct it and provide an explanation as to why it occurred.

Complete openness:

AI ought to be transparent about its operations. If it recommends a song or game, it should explain why it made that selection.

Confidentiality:

Artificial intelligence is obligated to safeguard your data. Your personal information, including your name, address, and other details, should be protected and not disclosed without your consent.

Security:

Artificial intelligence should be constantly tested to ensure safety. Self-driving cars, for instance, must be monitored as often as possible to prevent accidents. AI may be an excellent assistance if it adheres to five straightforward guidelines, ensuring that it is trustworthy, fair, and safe.

Ten AI Ethics

Artificial intelligence (AI) is becoming a big part of our lives. AI is everywhere, from intelligent assistants like Siri and Alexa to games and educational tools! However, with great technology comes great responsibility. The following are the ten crucial AI ethics students should understand in order to use AI responsibly and improve the world.

1. Respect Privacy: AI can collect a lot of information about us. Respecting people's privacy and not sharing personal information without permission is essential.

2. Be Honest: When using AI, always be honest about what it can do. Please don't pretend that AI can do things it can't, and always give credit to the AI for its help.

3. Use AI for Good: AI should be used to help people and solve problems. Think about how your use of AI can positively impact your community and the world.

4. Avoid Bias: AI can sometimes be biased, meaning it may maltreat some people. Always question the information and results AI provides and ensure they are fair to everyone.

5. Think Critically: Just because AI gives you an answer doesn't mean it's always right. Always think critically and verify the information before believing or sharing it.

6. Be Safe Online: Stay safe online using AI tools. Don't share personal information; be cautious about who you interact with.

7. Understand Limitations: AI is not perfect. It can make mistakes, so it's essential to understand its limitations and not rely on it for everything.

8. Share Knowledge: If you learn something new about AI, share it with your friends and family. Teaching others helps everyone understand AI better and use it responsibly.

9. Be Kind: When interacting with AI, remember to be kind. Treat AI with respect, just like you would with a person, and encourage others to do the same.

10. Keep Learning: AI is constantly changing and improving. Stay curious and learn about AI and its ethical use to become a responsible user.

• • •

Solved Short Answer Questions

Question 1: What does AI ethics suggest about how AI should treat people?

Answer: AI should treat everyone equally, regardless of their origin, appearance, or how they talk.

Question 2: Who is responsible if AI makes a mistake?

Answer: The creators and users of AI are responsible for correcting mistakes and explaining why they occurred.

Question 3: What does "complete openness" in AI ethics mean?

Answer: AI should be transparent about its operations, such as explaining why it recommends a song or game.

Question 4: How should AI handle personal information?

Answer: AI should safeguard personal information like names and addresses and not disclose it without consent.

Question 5: Why is it essential to test AI systems regularly?

Answer: Regular testing ensures AI systems, like self-driving cars, are safe and operate without causing harm.

Question 6: What does "respect privacy" mean in AI ethics?

Answer: Respecting privacy means not collecting or sharing personal information without permission.

Question 7: Why should AI be used for good?

Answer: AI should be used to help people, solve problems, and positively impact the community and world.

Question 8: Why is it essential to understand AI's limitations?

Answer: Understanding limitations is important because AI is imperfect and can make mistakes.

Question 9: What is a key reason to keep learning about AI?

Answer: Learning about AI helps you stay updated on its changes and ensures responsible and ethical use.

Question 10: How can sharing knowledge about AI help others?

Answer: Sharing knowledge helps friends and family understand AI better and use it responsibly.

About The Author

Dheeraj Mehrotra, a white and a yellow belt in SIX SIGMA, a Certified NLP Business Diploma holder, is an Educational Innovator, Author with expertise in Six Sigma In Education, Academic Audits, Neuro-Linguistic Programming (NLP), Total Quality Management In Education, an Experiential Educator, a CBSE Resource towards School Assessment (SQAA), CCE, JIT, Five S, and KAIZEN. He has authored over 100 books on computer science, AI, digital body language, NLP, quality circles, school management, classroom effectiveness, and safety and security. A former Principal at De Indian Public School, New Delhi, (INDIA), NPS International School, Guwahati, Kunwar's Global School, Lucknow and an Education Officer at GEMS, Gurgaon, with ample teaching experience of over Three Decades, he is a certified Trainer for Quality Circles/ TQM in Education and QCI Standards for School Accreditation/ School Audits and Management. He has also been honoured with the President of India's National Teacher Award in 2006 and the Best Science Teacher State Award (By the Ministry of Science and Technology, State of UP), among others. He has published over 100 books and developed 150 FREE EDUCATIONAL MOBILE Apps for the Google Play Store exclusively for Teachers, Students, and Parents. This work has been recognised by the LIMCA BOOK OF RECORDS and INDIA BOOK OF RECORDS as the only Indian to draw that feast. As a premium UDEMY Instructor, he has developed over 500 courses and caters to over 8 Lakh students from 180 countries.

Books By The Same Author

Scan Here!